# Reflections of the Moment

*by Arthur Weil*

# Reflections of the Moment

## Copyright © 2001 by Arthur Weil

For all inquiries or to order additional copies of this book, contact Arthur Weil, 208 Pala Avenue, Piedmont, CA 94611, aweil444@aol.com
Pricing: $5 per copy (25% discount if ordered directly through the author with no shipping costs)

Some images copyright www.arttoday.com

ISBN: 0-9676149-3-7

Printed in the U.S.A. by BookMasters, Inc.

# Acknowledgments

Thank you to Kandy Kidd, Jerome Kirk, Shirley Klein,
James Maiz, and Vicky McNail
for their help in proofing and reviewing the text.

*Special thanks to Seth Lepore for persevering in the completion of this
book. Yet again, your consistent work in compiling, editing, and
arranging this book cannot be appreciated enough.*

# Dedication

To all the ghosts of friends and family who are no longer here.

# Table of Contents

## Photo/ Sketch Art Credits

*Front Cover Photo*, Arthur at Donner Lake, California
*The Magic is You,* p. 1, Arthur and Lillian Weil at a charity dance
*Kosovo*, p. 5, Carbo San Lucas, Pelicans eating Swordfish
*It Will Get Better*, p. 8, statue by Emanuel Vigeland, Oslo, Norway
*Inner Symphony*, p. 22, Oakland Botanical Gardens, Bellevue Avenue
*Single*, p. 29, bronze sculpture by Henry Morre
*True Love*, p. 32, painting by Vincent Van Gogh
*Gum Remnants on a Tree*, p. 39, Tree outside of Ford's Theater
where Lincoln was assassinated
*If We..*, p. 45, copy of the Liberty Bell
*Packrats*, p. 52, Cigarette butts in ashtray
*Infinite Space*, p. 57, Lake Tahoe, California
*This Morning*, p. 62, Orangutan, Zoo, Washington D.C.
*Through My Ages*, p. 68, Arthur with friends, April, 1944, Chicago
*Youthful Folly*, p. 75, Jordan Weil (3and a half years old)
*Words to Heal*, p. 80, Lake Merritt bird sanctuary, Oakland, CA
*A Day in Numbers*, p. 85, Dinner at Lisa Weil's
*The Other Side of Nothing*, p. 89, Northern Scotland
*Within*, p. 92, Painting by post-impressionist
*Winners and Losers*, p. 97, Josh Steinhorn on rock climbing wall
*A Pedestal*, p. 102, Painting by post-impressionist
*Seeds of Poetry*, p. 104, Watercolor by Arthur Weil
*In the Senses*, p. 106, Painting by Vincent Van Gogh
*Blueprint*, p.113, Mobile by sculptor Jerome Kirk
*Burial Day*, p. 118, Painting by El Greco
*Accessories*, p. 122, Two hand posed, New Mexico
*When*, p. 128, Cabernet Grapes, Napa Valley, CA
*Give and Take*, p. 132, Photo of Lillian, Jeff and Judy Weil, 1959

The magic of this
      Book is you
Yes    you the reader
As you venture
Dream

Dance with my light rhymes
Your luck will turn
      Into action
 Your mind delirious
Ignited by thoughts
The power is within you!

Belief and deed in visions does spell action
Results are sure to follow
      For better or worse
      Fortune in thought
      Joy in behavior

Ecstatic in love of mankind
To read is to enrich the mind
Phrases into visions
Read – read – dare open your mind

So go ahead
Read a few rhymes each day
They were written
For unique you
By my delirious mind
With love and gratitude
In life – if not you
Who?

## A Question to Mankind

There is something diabolical about mankind
We are human, tender, yet often blind
Rationale, yet often act by instinct
Inside all of us the root
An animalistic urge at time so understood
Ready to attack, devour, emerge
Nostril keen taste, sharpened sight
Hormones dance and find their delight
Straight forward to suckle like a babe
Fill a devious urge with utter desire
To overpower, mast, bordering on rape
We must compete
Victorious annihilate and beat

Yet man, you and I
Of all creatures by God are christened  - human
Each of us a unique machine, 30000 genes plus,

To act by instinct, tempered by reason unashamed
Yet we unleash, cut our civilized rope
Often devastating anger, explosion, in conflict
Still we control, we cope, we try to overpower
In our fiendish act, diminish as we self-devour

A minute to admire and adore
The next minute so dominant, demanding war
So vex, so complex, ready to settle any score
Where will mankind head to next?
We humans climb an upward spiral
Profound in complexity, new inventions and new wars
Always with the best intentions
To our own future enter and shut open doors.

We, you and I, are God's gift
Very special creatures
Who challenge nature and self
Imbalanced, anxious seek for all to learn the golden Mean
Our gift of fantastic knowledge and experience
By all detected and now seen.
Yet the very clay of life that shapes us
To that life must return
Leaves us in torment wandering
Innocence overthrown – we burn
Life sentence gone – too late,
We can't return
Nor ask the why        that seals our fate.

### The Mystery of Life

every grand     playful adventure

        has its extremes        and censure

            broad-minded overlook

let excitement flair and cook
                dampen with                           your mores

values,
            even control     the deed in question

            devious brain the act       the bastion

                            you'll split adventure

    the soul     flirt with omnipotence   dance with the angels

                    dive to the ethereal   appearance and reality  in
question

        wounded        hurt

witness a spectacle     more   I am the actor the protagonist

                    absurd

lose love        adventure           friend

years hence debate

                            really never understand

The mystery of life eternally confronts

## Kosovo

They slay – then eat the flesh – conscience lost lost
The moral fiber and life's values tossed
When so much rests at the pinnacle of power
Swift, wise decisions by the hour
Two sides now play the game as leader steer
Both struggle, try to dominate and hold life dear

A pyric victory, perhaps
Wound heals as years do lapse
The titan's death dance
Over masses few escape by chance.

All in the name of religion or of "right"
Control and decimate with power and with might
Obliterate beastly, land and house
Uncivilized self-serving go, dominate, as men carouse.

Each side feels just      and in their hearts seem right
Religion, race turn into angry     futile    fight
All the peoples' powers subverted and subjected
All the laws, values of humanity neglected

G'd     why did you shape my world so perfect
Only to fall in disarray so that we must rebuild, and reenact
A new, hopeful, spiritual      harmonious state
Before we blow each other into smithereens

And self-destruct by any means despite the desperate pleas

Are we not unique, do we not search for inner peace?
Help us! Oh heavens find, let us rededicate new ways to heal
So that we proudly can proclaim fearful our fate
This peace-searching world of mine I say is real.
And please no more destruction
You the creator
What you have made
With no one to confess all obliterated
Too late, no scorn – let your children live
In struggle born

Too late.....too late

Never! Never too late !

*Challenge Adversity*

Each beam on us glistens
With heavens protection
Yet it is up to us to do
To plant, choose in each election
The juice of nature drink
As we challenge our adversity
In the fighting stance and fighting ring
Prove worthy with delight
For nature's victorious honor
Gives hope and
Makes things right

## Hands

Give your hand
Reach out to understand
The sensual clasp, unites, sensual, powerful
Electric – alive - so very much
Envelopes deep feeling, waving, warm

At this moment, you so special,
Two antennas telegraphing, we entranced
Two bodies meeting at extremities
Love and friendship message most advanced
To brain, from brain to body and my soul
Our hands entwined most heavenly
As if sweet golden honey drowns our appetite
Too good, too rich, ecstatic - wonderful

Strength of hand clasps, rapture
Tingling of the fingers nerves
Softness and vibrant feeling
Soon withdrawn – time, obligation
Pulls like tycoon, or hurricane asunder
Coupled our softness no more
We loosen our grip,
Must part for different shore.

Go, as my subconscious wonders: "When will we meet again?"
Shake hands, hold hands, clasp hands
So warm, so giving, tender
So tingling, mingling – most delirious
From hands to arms and lips the bodies merge
When will we ever meet again?
Deep impression caught,
New urge to touch again
Entwined in love's nest caught
Ingrained, encased within the body mind and thought.

## It Will Get Better

It will get better!

I have faith
I must do something about it.
Dare
Nothing is fair,
Everything
Has a value
I really itch, scratch temporary
Relief
Albeit damages
Each day brings more beautiful
Experiences to contrast with my anguish
If ONLY I could open my senses, receptacle
To receive
There's value in choice
More value in the doing
MY DOING!
It will get better!

Even more in doing    good and right

Try not to promise
I may disappoint a friend
Mostly yourself
Mind now focused
Determined
It's in the action- doing - doing
I'll get my greatest satisfaction
It may get worse
Before it will get better!


## Momentary Bliss

Better to love
Experience the pain
Than mourn alone
In dampness, dark and rain
Let all emotion reign
And contemplate the juice

Of bodies touching, meshing,
Gliding, probing
Dance of ecstasy
This momentary bliss
Of bodies merging with each kiss
Parting like clouds
The memory, the smile
Balls of joy and sadness
Brain buzzes as I sit
At the power
Of parting

## Complex

she thought of me

           a simpleton

    primitive,    a man

into sports    beer  coke

               would read a book

                         of sorts

more training in    romance

               to be desired

      More empathy     passions fired

    inventive  lovemaking

               more prescribed

Not ambitious enough    received what she bargained  for

     she was satisfied  or was she?

            her stimulation not exciting

most tired

        a memory lapse

      a rough recitation    Eyes ogle sexeliscious

           a short answer

but I am as complex    as she is    sitting on exploding

hormones   or imploding

         therein lies the rub

## Beyond Limitations

Don't you see it?
Relax. Lean back! Eyes closed
Breathe slowly – inhale – exhale
My body out in space looks down
Beyond my limitations
Into the aura of the cosmos
Into the vast chasm of the mind
As if in dream


The grey fibers under skull
Fabricating a web
Unique, man's genius into shapes and forms
Beyond – beyond the norms
Of man – the dreamer
The conceiver
Driven by some mystic force
Which stretches into the eons of space
I am the witness – the participant
Ignoring time, ignoring fear - daring
Pushed,
Break out of conformity
A timeless, endless space
Into the hews and shapes
Beyond belief – rainbow colors smattered
Into brilliance of greens, blues
Light yellow does reflect
Blinding bright pureness of the white
Sub-conscious          space
No teasing of the intellect

It's simply here. So am I

Don't you feel it?
Do you see it?

I see – I feel
I almost touch
Yet it touches me – all of us.

My imagination
Triggered
   Never figured
      No time to question – doesn't matter
Consumed with love
Taste – skim pinnacles,
Lap with fishes on the wide ocean,
Discarded conformity and chaste
Breaking the many layers
My mouth open with amazement
Gaping – accepting - mesmerized


Mind almost separate from body
Out of mind – spinning in a tornado touching clouds
Shattering free flow, unconfined
Abandonment, total, no criticism, no value judgment
Free traveler in total space visible – invisible
Real and not real
Subliminal the "Angst" and fear
The dream of hope, so close, so near
Now dances to the extreme

Touches, cavorts
Over curves into deep crevices
Exciting nerve and body rapture
Lifted from earth
Like phantom, heart and body
Now in spirit worth
Close your eyes
Relax       relax

Don't you see it?
Don't you see it?
I do
In the vacuum of space
A moment in eternity


## Choice

We owe much
All, and nothing to society
Our world
Wasn't our choice
We just grew up that way


## Maintenance in Friendship

Friendship has to be nourished
Like the garden
Sometimes we even
Need a disinfectant, insecticide
To kill the fungus


## Other-Wise

To be wise
Means to have
Suffered much
Aged, or otherwise

## Growing Pains

The blood festers in newborn
      In wretched pain
Cries hauntingly, suckling, innocent
      It must sustain
The precious mother's milk lapped up, lasts but so far
As a toddler mixes with his peers to spar

Live rich, a bitch, sans teeth, sans interlude
With pain in gums, new teeth protrude
Joyous vexed, perplexed the childhood years

Wanting, desiring in beginning years
      Sheltered, protected, in innocent tears
All life's a play before the magic age
      Elevates at ten or eleven, a new stage

We are men and women of goodness
      Awaited anxious for peace in heaven
      And yet we churn and boil
      The cauldron of hell
      $2^{nd}$ chance or none will tell
      Ready to explode and mix with earthy soil
Perturbed, concerned, jovial
      A challenge full of zest
Each day in awe in God and nature's help
      Delirious in search of rest, of peace within
Each day renewed, thankful to be blessed
      Nurtured – always in search
12 – now mature man or woman – give me a break
      Have not sown my seeds for goodness sake
Never satisfied like the succulent babe
      Ready to conquer horizons
Bathe in the zenith of hope and eternity
Grow – grow – until like dying rose petals

Shrinking withered falling onto - into the earth
Crossed from childhood into brotherhood of men
Shouldering responsibility again, again
Never to return to innocence, sheer play


## Secret Revelation

The body slighted
　　　　　Eager for communion righted
An inner urge to bond and mend
　　　　　Feelings of passion, love does blend
Spirit within spirit uplifted
　　　　　Am I so blessed to feel, am I so gifted?

Oh master of the universe
　　　　　Accept, open up my tainted body - nurse
My passion, anxious ready to explode
　　　　　Bless me, relive, relax, let me unload

Head toward heaven, hands uplifted
　　　　　Thankful for loving you, I have been gifted
Like Adam and Eve, the fingers touch
　　　　　I, too, seek love, solace in you so much

That other earthy love so touching sensual now instilled
　　　　　Over powering desire – empty and unfilled
Soothe me with secret revelation
　　　　　Inspire zenith of sensation
Though body age, the sigh and thrill of you within
　　　　　Protect me from blind passion into sin

If this last dance with searing pain in heaven
　　　　　My bread shall rise, bake and leaven
Like actor balance on the magic rainbow beam

I, the protagonist play out my angel's dream
I was innocent when born
        Now tarnished, imperfect, touch of scorn
Yet one last natural crush, shower of kisses, of sensual bliss
Thorough abandonment, embrace and kiss and kiss
Kiss the earth, curvaceous bodies now succumb
Transform to party celebration with its final romp.


## Apricots

Tasty Turkish apricots
With juice, tongue teased
Turn me into knots
Stewed, chewed
Orange color dried
My mouth is full of delights
Alright, alright
A bit tangy, tantalizing
My nostrils, tongue saliva full of joy
All because this small, dry apricot
Improved my mind and disposition
Why not?
That's what happens when you eat dried apricots

## Speed of Life

Magnetic waves

      Invisible, powerful – devastating

      span continents and space

Bolts of lightening speed

      connect the human race

Connect and do divide

      Communicate, fabricate, isolate

On visual and dimensional screens

      most fierce

Microphones, sound waves

      tease inner ears

Into my brain, your brain

      Sense, senseless do sustain

This paramount bundle, insatiable

      Information

Transmits, multiplied

      generated data

Digested, analyzed,

returned sooner or later

Yet, at its core,

mankind has generated

All this stuff – where does it come from –

How to absorb?

Multiplied still not enough

Spread seeds of thought – of questioning – of wonder

As information festers

in the corners of earth's child

An idea is nurtured, beamed to the satellite

Only to return scattered to the nooks

And crannies of our earth

In each mind so bright blossoming into light of freedom

To question – test – the truth – the word

Mind slaves now free to question alert

No dictator – ruler safe behind the walls of lies

Where does it end?   New knowledge heaped

Barely digested – no one can stop

Too many eager now to test it

What shape or form

Stored, cored, hated and adored

I dare think of the future worn

The genie out of bottle everywhere

Too much, too much

The more I know

I heave a ton of scorn.

The mind unchained - demand for justice, change, expression

I, too, jump on the bandwagon of free thought

Can you blame me?

Can you tame me?

So much to learn and challenge

Can I still trust

Can I still believe?

## To Grieve

Untimely, unwanted death     touches deep
          Yet vision of dear friend
                              and memory I keep.
Engulfed in anguish, pain I shed
Try to remove the heavy hurt
                              like weeping onion peel instead
Shed layer after layer
                    Friend do console – a layer
Time slowly healing – a layer
                    A heavenly prayer, a layer
Remembering the time we spend – a layer
                              Salty tears – lighten – a layer
Knot in my stomach     transfer to death – a layer
                              Skimming picture books and
memorabilia, a layer – videos – photo albums – a layer
Fulfilling wishes – layer    Visions of beauty in golden phases
               Voice image resonate in many places
Consoling others – a layer
               Building a memorial in thought     not
things – a layer


Each layer closer painful – agonizing
                    To find my new self
Each layer strips me to the core as mind's contortions delve
                    Full of compassion, love and
more
Torn, yet within impregnated vision of the one I do adore
Dead - why in vivid replica the face, the eyes still stare at me
The body motion all so real – I almost hear and feel the voice

Like the lines of stratification of an ancient canyon
               So too, each line depicts an era of our
friendship

Each onion ring another tear     new level of our bond
            Biting, consoling, diminish loneliness and fear.
            A true and scary vision – so imagined
I dare not forget the dear departed
            A balance between grief and hope,
good-hearted
For days and months, my dear friend's apparition
my delight
Awkward, different - mortal
            Life so fleeting, tenuous – never just
right
We are but babes,
            the helpless puppets in heaven's sight.

We are a tiny grain in world's great weal
Like all of life our pain diminish and we'll heal.
Let's change the word called "death"
Relapse of apparition, return dear friend
I will heal! I will heal!
I miss you dearly.

The scar remains forever!


*Forget*

Some are meticulous    never forget
I often forget     always regret
Then there are  things I'd rather forget
Can't erase them out of my head
Until my brain is so fully loaded
My guilt, anxiety    almost exploded
Best ease the pain    take you time
You'll be fine
Unless you're as forgetful as me

## Inner Symphony

Always a chance for reprieve
Renewal, rebirth in belief
When things are most bleak
Despite the deadly gloom
I prematurely feel interred in an eternal tomb

Conscious still I want so much to live
To take, to share, to love, to give
Body, membranes often not so willing
I am alive, only the devil problems do his killing

G'd knowing it is time and when
That is why the now, the here, I
      live again
With each breath, a precious flaring thought
Of beauty, faces, memories long caught
The symphony of nature's colors bundled
In fragrance treasured in my brain

Know that I love you, want to touch once more
The painting, music, books adore
Hear the child's laughter in it's
      innocence

As if all life a vision, a pretense

Last trip of painful joy
        to never land
We learn, we toil, sensations,
Some not understand
Omnipotent grandiose, hideous clouds
        obstruct
As we escape and win and call it luck

The soul breathed by the master soon
        recalled
Blasphemous, confront our maker
        most appetizing
We rue, why now, never to hear
        to see again
The anvil, act, electric, poison bolt
Erases breath and every pain


### True Writers

There are writers
There ARE writers
Straight from the cuff
Direct, blatant
Without snuff
Good honest stuff

Transmit electric thought
What brilliance has G'd wrought?
Sentimental, open and sincere
Pragmatic, loving, friendly dear
Their message sweet or acid criticism

With care and fare and author's dare
Lubricated, adulated, unabated
Flowery, imbedded within nature's call
The flora, fauna in foundation says it all

Then again
Weird, obtuse, shock value
Writers verbose profane
Thumb up your nose
Irregular thought borders
On the edge of the insane
Long shirked convention, evolution
No form, just words and space
Part like poisoned quivers in a rage

Then again, long never-ending writer
Polemic poetry, profusion seers
Religion, dogma, Karma, deep belief
Withdraw and pray, isolate relief

Our next computer driven world is poets on the go
Whitman, Shakespeare, Goethe, Frost
Their florid, fluent words
Renewed another age and day

Challenge, piercing biting words that never stop
Some poems rattle G'ds and institutions
Never to give up
Justice for every man/woman in our new age
Banner led by poets sensitivity and rage

## To Sleep

to sleep

       mind in nirvana

              spaced  - half erased

thoughts  phase away

           rest     less

            teasing and play


Subconscious      tense dream world

more rest     (some zest)

          foreboding thoughts

                      of love  of coitus

of conflict     unresolved

           contest  always at the abyss

        a moving chase  threatening
Tied, immobile, helpless, jolted into ecstasy

         layers of colors, faces, places

the morning ladder's rung

                    one      step         at         a
                                    time


                      don't believe the rhyme

life      is too harsh, too                          cross back


        somehow nature

                                          all want to boss

I am but one person

                        Eager     ready to awake

Haunted by dreams collective

              Stir up fears   unresolved   dark

                    The living lifeblood sucked



                        *Idiot's Laugh*

The idiot's laugh
His howl expresses
Infinite possibilities
As he walks in our shoes

## Man's Shadow

Grotesque over centuries
Men have plundered, raped
Robbed, abused in beastly fashion
Conquering the feminine mystique
And still do!

In the cavernous dungeons of their palaces
Walls cry out and echo the agony of the past

Driven      uncivilized
Teased by hormones – self aggrandizement
To propagate the race
Addicted to sex
Untouchable – the sons of rex
Hungry to self-satisfy desire
With blind strength and palpitating heart
Each continent, each civilization
Recount might over right, especially in sex
As we today encounter the complex
And do!

In modern times      in prison
Men still rape men
Subdued, released the sexual urge
With robust strength attack and surge

With such abandonment
Callous concern
Is it any wonder
That mankind denudes forests
Kills whales
Sprawling cities devastate the orchards
Unreceptive to the deadly hole in Northern Hemisphere
with ozone

Devastates forests,
Poisons rivers and streams
Chemicals and pesticides imbedded in
Farms and plantations
Rapes natural wonders with callous stupidity
Causes nature's imbalance
Rueful avenging by heaven
Clones – genetic aberrations
Unlawful, cruel attack
The rape of ourselves
We who have reason
We who can teach sensitivity
We, of a chain of ancestors of scholars
We who cherish and protect
For our progeny now
Observe the
Wanton destruction of our own soil
The retro-evolution into the womb of time
And of all living things
Ignore history, discard wisdom
When will we revolt in juxtaposition
Between civility and fiery balance
And end the rape that destroys
All that we believe in?
Or return to the beast
From hence we derived
And melt to nothingness
Extinct– before Adam

*Single*

Your base of security in childhood
Provided love and care from motherhood
Surrounded by family and friends
A rich and happy life you could depend
Severed from the family tree
Fend for yourself on not so solid ground
Anguish, uncertainty and isolation found
Too busy to apologize and make amends
Forget about the        L
Which I will spell      O
                        N
                        E
                        L
                        I
                        N
                        E
                        S
                        S

Derived      now  single

into world at birth

touch of mirth

Some of us isolated     exist in painful  loneliness

Eternal sleep – travel in hearse

You curd
          Don't be absurd

Everyone is lonely at times

                It's ok,          it's a friend

You follow your agenda as you please

Can we connect     in due time

Aren't we all family?


## The Fly

I remember
As a child
The buzzing, busy, bothersome fly
Teased me at the kitchen table
Brushed my ear
Dared, visible with the humming sound
Was it the light, the smell of food
Circling, diving – buzzing near cheek,
Even sitting on my plate

Don't know why
Irritating, watched by my eye
Quick with practice
I am about to catch
The naughty teasing fly
Patiently I waited
From the corner of my eye
The fly I spy
Where the fly landed
Conspicuously arrogant it landed
Slowly, ever so slowly
Into position
Observing fly's every move
Now my open hand
Follows the take off
Hand follows
The flies rear

Then as the fly
Takes off
Quick as lightening- open hand follows
In one swoosh  - quickly close my hand
My hand now does
Its stuff!
In my closed hand
Still fully alive
The struggling
Tickling fly
I feel
Should I squash it?
Take it outdoors
Open my hand
To freedom
Now it's real
Now fly – please stay away

Love yourself
As you love life
Believe: "I'm special."
Endearing
Honest
Curious and compassionate
Well appearing
Inside in soul
In our palpitating heart
In vibes to others
Love and kindness
Sometimes smart
Feet on earth
To celebrate
Life
Your life much worth
Your genes and chromosomes
Special, exuberant
Team up
Each moment exquisite
For happiness you seek
In this love
Narcissus

Touch and suck
Open to the world
Peculiarly unfurled
I love you, too
You woman, man
You bend     old
You     innocent child
Love you with sensations
Not wild
As my spirit
Meshes with yours
You accept my love
As I hold your love dear
We build palaces of dreams
Discover cures for ills
Cautious heed
In doing and the deed
As we travel at speed of a rocket jet
Cuddle, loving in warm bed
Calm with love bewitched
Touch of annoyed anger
Feed the world with peace
Marvel the magnetic force of reason
To slow man's craft
No more devour neighbor's goods
Live with the temporal
Grateful – special unique
Our goodness explode
Spread the seeds of love
In every mode

Spiritual within our limited space
Confined by unlimited, unselfish love
Encounter endless horizons
Blinding beheld by earth's beauty
Encapsulated in the mind

I love myself
My mind in yours
Entwined
As again we mesh
I feel your every tentacle
Tender and electric fibers
Hug, rub our tender flesh
As we beam
On lifelines
Real and most extreme
All sound is music to the ears
All laughter cries
Mighty feasts come and go
All vision ever changing
Transformed
In mind so floating
Arranging
My body quivers with delight
Nirvana inside me
This day and night
Things like atoms split asunder
Yet joy, will, soul we find down under
Love
Pure love to struggle and subsist
                  Eternal, loved by angel
                  I've been kissed

## Subtle Expressions

there is poetry
                    in all of us

the wrinkles in our face

                    the cheerful smile


    agile walk, staccato talk

              the mystic odor we exude

Our whine, wince, laugh – glorious voice

         our animation  our sneers and cusses

                vividly           express
sensation

    shock of sad news    The resonance of our voice

           salty  tears absorb

       listen to the blues

the way we work,  artistic cooking   delight in eating

          Abhor much – yet touch, soft gentle kiss


Eyelids wink       self appointed generous gift

       News of new child, of well earned prize

Crooked bend of the old man picking up dropped keys

Each a touch on the canvass of life

each unique

accomplished feat

There's poetry in all of us indeed

## Silent Thunder

Out of deep utter silence
 I sit at the corner of my bed
A melancholy moment
Come with me,
A lifetime in a thousand sparkling useless thoughts
Flash vivid personages the celluloid of past
Problems unsolved
As I sit on the corner of my bed

In silence mingle
Perturbed and occupy
Fear and frolic
My eyes closed
As I sit at the corner of my bed

My ears tingle
My body in rapture
Like silent thunder
Rambunctious
Images appear
Of father mother

Of placid lakes,
Foolish fantasies
Eerie, long departed
Yet so alive this moment
As if held in this silent space
Called mind
Called mine
To irritate and shine
As I sit at the corner of my bed

Most, the vision of old love
In bloom, in trace
In charming embrace
Prize winning dance
As I sit at the corner of my bed

Then the bell or phone rings
I am left
In the shock
Of reality
As I sit at the corner of my bed


*Even Giants...*

Love and kisses tantalize
Beware when to your surprise
Blindly overwhelm all
Creating their own zenith
                    Even giants fall

Schizophrenia, disjointed muse
With human intellect
Puts thought puzzle pieces
Life flashes on imaginary boards
To frame life pictures, linked
Intertwined with subconscious thought
I've seen and tasted much
But this is stranger than fiction

So here, the angry jolted love
Destitute, downtrodden, ego smashed
Turns pure love into ravenous hate
Torment of revenge, leading
To self-destruction
Stranger than fiction

The woman with babe in
Fury finalizes her decision to
Part from her unfaithful man
Threatening in anger
Despite poverty
The consequences of sustenance
Stranger than fiction

The computer hacker, fatigued burned
Out kisses the boss good bye
Breaking chains
Freedom without
Stranger than fiction

Having another joy to fill in letdown
Void after much intense work
The middle-aged daughter reprimands
Her old parents for their failure to provide

A happy childhood
Heaves blame and false accusations
Why must we vent and spew
When living now so exciting and so true.
Stranger than fiction

These are sample summaries
Of our stranger than fiction stories

*Gum Remnants on a Tree*

I felt numb
I saw all these remnants of gum
Outside the entrance of Ford's Theatre
In Washington D.C.
Where the multitude honors Abraham Lincoln
Who was assassinated inside
But first the chewing gum must commemorate
The tree in front of the entrance
In all its glorious colors

## Subliminal Messages

We bounce off sentences
Messages and thoughts
Transposed, transferred
Echoed, interpreted
Digested, regurgitated, chewed
Immense power of the world
Infant and elder
Inflow, outflow
Thoughts through words

I love you
I hate you
Help me
Come....leave

I think

A profusion, a man of words

Multiply this with our reading
World without word and symbol
Is the world of cats and dogs
Tower of Babel depressed mankind
Too many tongues
Which we encounter daily
And often do not understand

## Nakedness

Born innocent and naked
Raw, gooey, crying
I now feel guilty, foolishly naked
It is by choice
Unadorned, misshapen, naked
The shower refreshes
As I rub loin, buttocks
Shoulders, neck
Glance at my lifetime anatomy
It's only things
Like legs, toes
Maybe a glance into the mirror
Not real, not the same
Not the sprite me of yesterday
My mind now active, too busy
To dwell on yesterday
Or nakedness
The freedom of no clothes
Shuttered, naked
Soon to cover all
Put me back into my shell
For I shall leave the world as I came


## Our Legacy

Our legacy lies in how
We have lived
How we live now
How our children, friends
Reap the fruit of our deeds

## Heatwave

The heat of a hot summer, sweaty day
Pours forth in many forms
Uncomfortable irritant to man and mind
Hair conditioned cooler, I can find
Antiperspirant, fan, ice-cream all help
Go into the cool of the cave or subway
To escape, survive
Keep my sanity yet momentarily
Give me ice, tell me where I am

Burning less, body's thermometer adjusts
G'd so natural
Self-evident in pores of mesh
Chest and face
Exhausted and pesky
Warmer and warmer

Heat irritant in brain
The hormones rattle and sustain
Swell up, demand
Sometimes gyration, frustration
Vent love and anger

The sweltering heat
Pressing, obsessing

Bees buzzing, flies irritating
Dogs with tongues aching for thirst
Unabashed dancing
The hot maiden went mad
The sparks in configuration
Cinders and hell
Consuming all in black eerie fashion
Proclaiming disintegration of my earth

Until the heavens shower a cool breeze
Save us undeserving sinners
We suddenly forget- it's hot, it's hot
As I crawl into my safe egotistical shell

As if nothing ever happened

## *Squeaky Dog*

I hear the tiny, squeaky dog bark
Fright, alert, past midnight, what a lark
A yelp, repeated twice or more
The world asleep ignored the pooch
A barking bore

Perchance the dog had scared the cat and rat
Or simply made himself feel glad
At least I heard the tiny mutt
Go back to sleep
I am a tired lot

## Decisions

Some of us so decisive, so sure
Yet I wonder how to weigh the unknown?
Anxiety, wait exhausts
Fork in life's road
Have climbed the mountaintop
Which is the best way down?

I find it hard to decide
Which card to play
Which rule is right
With budget what to buy
When to tell truth, when the white lie
When I met a maiden fair
I pine, demure, love struck
She leaves for yet another
I am out of luck

Conscious or my subconscious
I do decide each detail and routine
From picking shoes to shocking colors
When my stock is out
I simply let 'em holler
What a shame
Too many older play that game
Each hand held not the same
And that is the great "enticer"!

## If We ...

If we could hear the bell of time
Awaken in us great adventure in our prime
The bells most wondering freedom's spirit brings
Accepted by our being sings
Proclaims us special, human, kind
The striking bell within and all around.
A wondrous, mind teasing soul-searching sound

If we could just be trusting
Be not be deceived and ready busting
But infinitely more patient
Witness the magic of resolve, revolve

If we could be clairvoyant
The future begs but be not scared
If we could stop, replenish and recharge
Gain precious self-directed time

If we could be that surgeon

Who could add an ear or nose
Or amputate our fears and misconceptions
Catch, relish in that creative moment
Before it dissolves evolving in new challenge

If we could eat less but taste more
Relish that special taste for a long, long time

If we could but forgive
But not forget
Then forgive again without absolution
Charter in desired new direction

If we could crack 100 smiles
Bubbly live in the positive upside-down world
Yet underneath the pain of omission
Of neglect and constant derision

If we could play our own soft music
Take the time to listen
Captured by melody and tone
Enamored, fascinated all alone

If we could love by touch and taste
Ride on the spirit most unfazed
Catapult in deep embrace
Consume the aroma, passion of this place

If we could alter our value system
If we could relive, re-experience the good
And in athletic shape skillfully pass on the ball
With hope, early rise to hear the bird's first call.

If in the mirror we could see the truth
Viewed from a thousand angles – still see same truth
And in the mirror feel the weight of soul

Of what I am, and what you are
And what is right reject the devil, follow shining star
And with all strength proclaim and act
Dare the unyielding weal of opportunity
And walk away – head held so proudly
That if my mother, my father could see me now
Their soul, their spirit burst with pride and joy

If – those two letters – IF

If we could but save and spend
And have some left until the very end
With joy of folks and fellowship and kin
Open our hearts and let the sun shine in

If we could mediate so that all fighting stop
Disbanding army no need for police or cop
And let us pray, each to his own
Great Gods of nature, each in our dialect in different tone

If we could meet – just now
And kiss and love and hug
I, grateful in the act, would show you how
Close, most intense, exciting, but do not call it love

If we could turn the time-clock back
Sorry I can't, nor will I break my neck.
Close my eyes,     things not what they do seem
    An apparition, foolish hope portrayed in sparkling dream
                    Not satisfied, but thankful
                    If we could merge the act and I
                    In short – its deed and doing
                    Why not try?

*Where is where?*

Misplaced or lost
                    Disgraced, mind emptied    tossed
Where is my precious memory
                    I knew I had it. I can see can visualize
But where is it?

Where is the chirp and whistle of the bird
                                        Here, desolated cold
not heard
Where is the playful children's song
                    Retired, convalescent, they do not belong

Where is the politician's promise kept?
                    Where is the where love and I have often
slept?
Where are the rich, star-studded hills?
                    Ugly space where row upon row of houses
fills
Where is the grey of future exciting anticipation?
                    Where is the world at work towards peace
and preservation?

I am concerned
I feel helpless
I am alone.
Will they really find me?
Will I find them?

## Weekend News

Bad news, sight and sound
They do abound
Volcano blown or forest fire
Shootings, plane crash – all expire
Perspective, irritant receptive
Your choice
Gloom and doom can be the omen of better
Be it great loss, defeat or tearful letter

Take a long moment     refocus and blot out
Smell flowers, walk, exercise
Dispel destroy     why vegetate and pout
No matter what, there is a heaven and a sky
There is a solid tempered floor, no one will die

Yet!

So why cajole, stew, fret
To all things - there is a solution
Humans unpredictable, turn the table
Progressive evolution
I want to joke, laugh
Work and toil ahead
To share, be liked, reward
Proud to make my own bed

The vibes from goals and positive deeds
Prove more fruitful if fulfilled
As we meet our needs
So you in darkened alleys scratch and whine
Touch hope, get up – march - join the crusade
Unselfish save our planet – most divine

Be a doer, a getter
> For sure you'll survive
> So will posterity
> All life be better


## Asleep in Love

There was not much I could do about it
I love her and such
The human drive and feeling fit
I sought her voice, her touch

So I fall asleep in love
Infatuated, lonely, longing thrust
There is so much, much more above
A joint embrace, renewed courtship now a must

Is it still possible, am I so vain
Here now, where is she
Must see her now again
My anxious drive, so devastating true

For now good night
To sleep, to dream, she in another world
Will rest and calm soon make it right
New challenge imagination, her vision is unfurled
As I see her silhouette by my side

Soon unfold the spirits
The ghost of yesterday is now
Her apparition, smile
Her sexy, most inviting style

Why does my mind dwell on her
Am so overcome
By one so dear and close
Pillow next to me – empty – begging


Reality trounces my apparition
Never to touch or kiss her ever,
Or feel arms and body most entwined with mine
Nature and G'd has seized my heart
Only pictures, memories and spirit creep beneath
My skin into the recesses of my mind
And she shall be my lifelong partner still.
                    And she shall be my lifelong partner still


*First Sign*

If you scratch heaven
        Challenge God
Lightning and the devil
        Will measure you at the gates of heaven
        Then come closer down to earth
Share with me your unearned fortune
Pulling you down into the abyss of time
Escape from purgatory
        This being your first sign

*Packrats*

Packrats (insecure) save all
Someday to use

       Sentimental
          Can't let go

Discard      Would break my heart

To sell? maybe          not to give away

Might need   that  toy, that chest   another      day

Too many shoes
Old clothes      pins   pictures – broken gadgets

                         Clips

Stationary   boxes of receipts  old tents

Many things needless have more than one

Outdated books    read over    years ago

      Cannot part with things    yet

When I will be old and sick
Too late – get rid

                     Discard

And I along – forgotten soon

      What a dirty trick

And I will join the heap of unnecessary baggage

Or hidden in the corner of some other packrat's rendezvous
But not by choice

### *Impeachment*

Impeachment with reason and
        resolve
The testimony devastating, the law
        broken
He, the beholder and guardian of the law
Lied, purged the personal
        that's the flow
No stealing, no wars, fantastic leader
Cheated on his wife, covered up
        lied to the nation and the reader
Caught sent regret, admitted shame
Censure, reprimand, diminished his
        fame
Still he's not infamous, vindicated
To world and child to lie is wrong
Deny the lie, get caught now plead
        a tragic song
Mercy and forgiveness are now the
        masses choice

The senate, solemnly now votes
        must listen to their inner voice
Bravo great pleader, Mr. President
Your knowledge, perseverance in the people
Do approve and assert
Your speeches, legislation and divisiveness resent
A gem, tired talent hard to replace
Plead guilty, move on
        pertain in any case
Why should man who has
        100 victories
Be soon removed with failure of but one
We on the stage, tradition soon
        often leader remover
        political life undone
No finish line, Mr. President
The nation's millions bid you well
        defect
A well deserved second chance
You are their friend, cooled off
        a close and warm man
Under the stars and heaven will all know
A trust that's broken is a heavy blow
Still friend, doer, leader
        most of all
Win over those who vote for you
Finish your term, never again beseech
        your call
For you have won and lost
Impeach for lying is a higher cost
Go back to work, meet with your cabinet
From now on be more careful
        with whom you go to bed.

## The Boundaries of Mankind

The boundaries of mankind
Made by mankind
Where to live, what to eat
How to dress, control, delete
Polite custom, what to say
In each situation
A special way

How to blow your nose
To kiss, to pose
How to respect
Guilt or neglect
Each stage so set
Even how we sleep on ground or bed
Ingrained in childhood
Like a mysterious code
And if we veer from it
Guilt and self-punishment

Yet new ideas and creative mind
New cars we choose to steer
Endless solution and selection
Yet only we decide in which direction
If we land, new vistas and abode
Our talent always learning as we carry our load
Boundaries within our own confines and limitation
We stretch, exceed them in mild moderation
Our genes and heritage and stimuli
Our brain depends, goal to succeed

These platitudes into action now transform
Use your ingenuity, be shaker –maker
Excel and overcome the norm

If in your travels and travail
You will succeed and best potential hail
Be thankful for each and every day so right
Use all your powers, appetite
For life is short, so short, do it without delay
So much to do, to see each day
                    Pace yourself – measure your sojourn
                    You can't do it all


## Morning Toiletry

I shower, washed myself with diligence
I dried
I felt something impure
*Me*
Shaved, teeth brushed
It was something else
I haven't cleaned my mind yet
And now you know what it was


## When Nothing Makes Sense

Sometimes when
        Nothing makes sense
I get up
Go to the other world
        And celebrate

## Infinite Space

Time knows
Silence - unspoken language
Fills miniscule parts in space
Air and the unseen waves
No vacuum unseen – through microscopes - meters
Messengers transfixed in space
With tongues, bodies real things
To be felt – heard answered

Brown mountains
Encrusted dark blue green oceans
All to fill the empty space

Space every where
Eternal absorbed
Disintegrated
I am writing in ghostly space
Can you read me?

I sit in     space
Surrounded by     space
Entombed in space
Breathing – sorbing – conjecturing

Unseen, invisible unending space

The lightning cuts, strikes
Teases, reverberates with a thunderous crackle
Ending in a vibrant shaken roar

We tiny little human beings  - and compared to the cosmos –
we are tiny
So infinitesimal in relation to my surrounding
Strut, pace, jump      and fly in heavenly – earthen space

No, I cannot be indifferent to space
Every move, every breath, every creation about
Takes place in the space about
Respect in awe my space
For only in death
Take up space
But only if body and earth return
To the gasses of birth

I can give up some space
    Enveloped     by      space
    Move jauntily about
Always occupying
Our homes    our boxes
Cities taking     space
A whole civilization reveling in space
But there is          more          of it
What if – if not where nature, where oceans?

Up and down

Left
Right

                                        Right

Mankind lives, consumes in space

No vacuum infinite – eternal

Just a wild play land of space
For Gods

Take me
I'll still leave vibrations

In holistic forum

I wonder

If I can get some old space back

Where the confluence of man and nature meet

And the struggle for peace

For survival begins

Somewhere in space

Yet earth is our battle ground

## Overwhelming Fillers

I seldom finish anything
Start the new
Escape, ignore
In frustration veer away
The bills, letters, cut outs
Articles all stare at me
Demanding
Sometimes I forget – on purpose

Now understand
Guilt! I want to run for office.
The glare of the TV screen
Loud blast and conversation
The speakers, the FM music
A cacophony of loud sounds
So deafening on ears like mine

Midnight raid on fridge
Stuffed, overate
No cure
The TV
3 newspapers
Financial quiz, health tips
All converse, all converge
Causing more confusion in my life
Isn't it time for all of us to share
No wonder that I seldom finish anything

## Persistent Cold

The cough drop between tongue and teeth
Throws off saliva soothing sweet
Mellows the throat, occasional squeeze
Mostly tickles, just a tease
Only rest and nature will do healing
This cold turned me into a helpless kitten
Our God is now revealing
Dwarf, every manual in our space
Gets a cold
Warning when and where to hide our race
No one is told
Cold now an awful surprise
Makes you appreciate your body
Clever yes, but not too wise
Just hope the common cold is not a flu
Then all your friends depart
You are through
Tired fatigued – never seems to end
As if the punishment from heaven sent
You feel sad, with time left to heal
Just hope the cold is not the flu so real
Once cold is gone
I better do catch up
I have double fun
Hard to remember how miserable I was
In hell, the other side of OZ

## This Morning

Who will I be today?

Grey light defused

      Distant prattle, rattle – nature

The morning brain     as I wake

Car noise outside

        The silence broken   beckons
Busy day – surprising

       Energetic day

Must I arise so soon?

So much to do,

      to see   to smell   gently touch

Olfactory glands urge

      for cereal eggs, juice

Eyes peruse the pillow       open magazine

      drawers - underwear spilling out

To pad the naked body

Shower bath, perfumes soap

            Enveloped in the steam

    Jerkily brushed, awakened pain, hair pulled

The radios TV now do disturb and pressure

      Resound new warnings, calamities catastrophes

  Events beyond control emotion

scream of awesome disaster       Or political drama

Begging demanding workday

        Too busy - involved
No time to retreat

        Too much at stake - life!

    The mind just half-awake

    Life beckons

## Reflection

I looked into his eyes
A smile, relaxed some wrinkles, a surprise
Well-groomed, wavy long soft hair
Silvery interlopes, reveal touch of age, some despair
The nose, a bit larger     prominent     protruding
So noticeable, pronounced, not easily eluding
Red solid tie, could be more even centerfold
I see, grandeur symptoms as he's getting old
Shoes polished, heels now need repair
Is he too busy, careless, doesn't care?

Complains, a bit grouchy, is he late?
So many things he does berate
Moves a bit slower, even stops a bit
Tries to tell jokes, mature, a touch of wit
Few yawns, agile, does reflex
Eyes sparkle, with libido and wanton sex
Too early to betray his age
When he was younger
Must have been the rage

I look now closer, sadly must divulge
Still keen he added weight, the bulge
No resignation, yet concern
An agile dancer waiting for his turn
Serene, a touch of loneliness
Involved, intense, a caricature of stress
Complex, determined, stubborn you can tell
I know him, yes I know him far too well

Memory glands have lapses most disturbing
Free awkward thought like spilling flood observing
The joy to be alive, to meet this day
Hurry – get going – relish work and play

Alone, I see him in the mirror now
Or you as years flee, candles snuffed
I honestly can tell – it's me and how!
I honestly can tell - -it's me and how!


## Surviving The Elements

The earth absorbs it's own
In the cycle of weather
Erosion and fire
As we live on top like an onion skin
Above the firmament, the clouds
And gasses which shield against the ozone
I cavort on this crust
Abundance of nature
Much dust and waste
Is swallowed up
Changing constantly
Ever fluent, not forever


## The Doers

Some ask for nothing
Others for all
In silence the doers
Help shape the world

## Too little/Too much

Where to draw the line?
Too much       too little
Overpriced       under-priced
Eternal love or       one-night stand
Abstinence or fully immersed
Overeat or starve
Too much involvement – not enough
Over-active – borderline of laziness
Penurious – or spend it
One more time – or enough
Self-involvement or freely sharing
Ignoring – caring
Belief – or disbelief
Love or stagnated feeling


Fool
The golden rule
The position of the earth does change
Man's horizon somewhat out of range
Or fool to be richest, best
There's always someone better
Better than the rest

Yet to excel, surpass or underachieve
To be devoted and believe
Destroys the need for cheating and the thief
Let yourself go, exercise
To pre-announce, enjoy       surprise

To break up or to make amends
Less enemies more friends
Neutral or in-between
To disappear or to be seen

Careless and dirty or
Spick and span

To celebrate or abdicate
To rise or fall
To hear the call
Blindly hear nothing
Nothing at all

To be a lowly miser or charitable giver
Support the cause or jump into the river
Sacrifice and pay the debt
To live as imbecile or be well read
Dissolve, ignore be most responsible to the core
To dress appropriate or dress offbeat, cause sensation
To melt with cool or stubborn renegade seek my ovation
Hard up for what is right
Avoid the easy wrong in flight

Sit down again or get up
Self-control or the wild outburst of a raging pup
Feign ignorance or advocate vow to improve
Collect the prize and donate funds as I behoove

Infinite lines illustrative are just a token
Like life – they can be bent and broken

I hear thunder, heaven's noises
We, on earth have many choices
Have many choices

unknown we've shared and cared

I thank you for your invitation

we, you     I unique
                 our generation

one of revolution
          depression
            poverty
                   the melting pot

we witnessed the advent
          of madmen

Stalin     Mussolini     Hitler     Tojo

we survived 12 million     2 fronts

were you born yet     I the actor in the play

Cold War

Students hiding under desks for shelter

                                                        Korea
Vietnam

suburbia
                    the advent of cities

                        recovery of our energy



                            the computer age
                                jet age
                                TV age

open our doors to millions

                Hungarian refugees
                Russian Jews
                Central American immigrants
                Vietnam boat people
                 Ethiopians, Haitians, Nigerians
                 Cubans, Irish
                        survived narcotics, dope

                    booze
                            new tranquilizers

            new in this speculative age

IPO's
401 K's

we're cloning

we live longer

(perhaps too long)

we are our brother's keeper

don't even have time for brother
or our own kids

the abundant age

still 40-50 poverty

think, know more
are better off

the abundant age

traffic jams

diets        fast food

mutant food
in all seasons

Avalanche of coke, crack, Aids

Of protest – isolation – change

70

Rap, hard rock, music videos, video games

                    Disneyworld   6 Flags

          remote this    and that

       microwave, alarm
                 fuel-efficient cars,     never enough

Microsoft 3 – 6    Compac – Intel – Dell – stock trading - Vegas


          still have parks
                     pollution

    eco-system

escape to the safety       of the suburbs

          big house

               simple yard

reaching my hands to heaven


         who is this wise, worn generation

*Who will...?*


Life dissolves
Into the fate of ashes and gases
Love's destiny  - unless we tame exploding population

We are the struggle of the sperm
That meets the waiting egg
Selective impregnation – magic - life
Fight extinction - reproduction – devastatingly too much

Welcome to the world's population boom
Six billion – seven billion – most below 30 years
To the edge of poverty – war and envy
Reinvent mutation, genes dare reproduce life itself

Who will feed? Who will clothe? Who will tame the hungry masses?
Malthus – the increment of humans will decimate the globe
Fly beyond the gravity of the earth
Struggle to build, invent each generation

A new creation
We are essential to rejuvenate the world
We eat, devour just a tiny piece of earth
Hence all our senses, burn destroy forests

Fumigation, contamination
Poisonous gases
Species extinct
Society imbalance – out of sink

Grow, grow  - we think we learn to cope
Cut the umbilical rope
Just like our ancient ancestors

The church declares all life sacred – so it is
But if our existence wee threatened y a deadly pest
We'd protect our way of life, our very nest

Long forgotten – yet fraught with danger
Careful – lest we devour each other
                    Which obviously we are doing


### Raspberry Candy

Crinkle noise as I unwrap the red dyed candy
I crave the sweetness, saliva tongue lick dandy
My tongue and teeth delightfully toss the bon-bon all about
The fruit-filled goo excites, melts in my mouth, I pout

Soon the last bit of raspberry, sugar in my mouth reduce
To a tiny, clinging, chewy ball I now produce
The nostrils send delightful aroma to the brain
Addicted to the taste I do inhale again

My tongue, my mouth, my gums a raspberry red
Better than blueberries, or boysenberries
The deep, rich red is so inviting
Texture of small berries so exciting

Alas, the juice, the goo now so minute
As I press, lick and try not to be rude
Too much, so bad for teeth and temperament
          Too late for now, I ate it all, it's gone and spent

          Now that I have tasted raspberry that I idolize
What succulent inviting morsel will be my next surprise?

## Missing Love

The pillow next to me so empty, yet so off
In deadly peace at AM, where is my missing love
I touch, perceive the emptiness, know she's not there
Eyes closed I see an angel escorted by a dove
This part of my life an empty fair.

Why did you leave me
Why did the lord, my other love, deceive me
In old age paired, you faded first
Now I am numb, miss little food, just quench my thirst

Lights on, your half of bed I see a missing ghost
Now holy space, imbued with love the most
Were I to touch you, kiss, share warmth once more
Whisper loving messages that I most adore

Where arm would reach to gently touch caress
Your shape and image clear I must confess
Yet warmth, inviting I do miss
Bend over form and body for a tender kiss

You are still with me so
I will see and feel you forever
The night deceiving young
Will I see you again
Piece of my heart missing in deep pain

*Youthful Folly*

Spring forward little one
Feel the wind-blown leaves brush your cheeks
Worship the moon and in between the sun
Know he who dares, and he who seeks
Will experience     will find
An indifferent impersonal kind

Innocent little one
You are too busy having fun
Go play, hug, test
Throw the ball
Protected in your nest
Play with our building blocks and toys
The realm for you so varied choice
Dare you leave before your time
The devil's itch, reality from mine
The bridge from innocence
To a real world far too soon unfurled
Curing, curing, enticing demented
Don't challenge it yet little boy
Leave alone the world, be not be envious, resentful
Treasure your freedom, admire each pearl

The new tingling candy taste,
The tangling licorice piece does curl
The swollen lips and titillating tongue
When you awake, no need for haste
Each move reveals a step on ladder rung
How long will nature keep you chaste
All day deep teasing joyful feeling now revealed,

Unsealed into the night – sleep deep
In present haunting beautiful relaxing heat
Tomorrow music mine to listen and cherish and to keep
As I listen I thank you so grateful and true you little one
In innocence revel in your youth
Before the grown up world holds you to accountable


### This Freedom

Freedom is more than a feeling
A spirit
A bird circling above the earth
In self control
A hiker on an alpine meadow
A lover deep in ecstasy

Feeling is neither right nor wrong
Feeling *is*
And our freedom of choice
Is one of our greatest gifts

## Inner Turbulence

I must be deft
to fight sleep
alert   awake       the next several  hours
unaffected euphoria
extreme humility


then a flu, a cold
so brazen bold
(inside) my chest
my breast, my brain ignited


uneven   irrational invited


when once  a world of hope, so calm


now a bit weird, balm


enormous disorder, weather pattern
up and down turn, unstable


the violent storm does part  so ably


settles, more tranquil
a new silence arouses the sky


reading truth from lies
knowing we are alive


this family intact


as we rebuild
man and nature do renew
inner cells die

New cells shape – the norm
Appreciation of our work

the new ideas   new forms
Excited follow new successful plan

living long lives     as best we can

## Stooping and Sinking

Too often we blame ourselves
Adversity hides between the innocent and unsuspecting elves
Strikes good and evil women and men
Destroys their aspirations, lifelong wishes

Self-guilt, self-torture, blame
It's nature's teasing deadly game
The mid-life solid, earned the prize
The devil's work, a dismal aura of demise

Oh heaven, why the innocent in torrent brew?
They're schooled, they've built, now all asked
Terminal illness unsuspected
Jobs, friends lost, to the gallows now elected

Shocked, that this great leader, we suspect
Just like the fainting princess is life wrecked
Through famine and bad luck
His/her life, hope has gone amuck

Is there no justice, keeper of the scale
Can good deeds, loyalty and honor still prevail?
Or is infection, virus, cancer cursed
Gambling, denial, justified to steal another's purse

Mankind stoops so high and sinks so low
Becomes its own villain of this tragic show
Damage done, belated remorse, regret
Now wallow in self-guilt ridden mental bed

Oh maker of the ghost and soul of life
Restore some pleasure, rejuvenate my drive
That joy and deed amend of days ahead
That once again I love and do instead

As refreshed I start my chores
My senses pleasure be creative, mold deeds with great force
Once again do laugh and smile
Treasure my day so thankful in my special style

## Miracle

We each have our own value system
To match ours with our partners
Still talk to each other
That's the real miracle

## Tolerant

To be tolerant of something
One doesn't have to like it
Just to let it exist
Maybe they are tolerating me

Flow, fly move gracefully
      Across uncharted space
Free inhibition dance, jump
      Spring
Freed animal of human race
Escape confusion, chains that tie
      our mind and grace
Oh joy of movement, leaps and love
Witness freedom below within and far above
Move with your miniscule tentacles and nerves
My arms flinch      heavenly I pray
For gentleness, for goodness and faith
As I dance most endearing
      Romantic in this place
I want the world my wound to heal
      To soothe
I echo tunes of harmony
      From my confined small
      Earthen booth
      Hence wings into the air
Just listen, listen to orchestra of nature
      With its fury and peace – always the beat
Listen to the magic of the valley
      Full of rustling trees
Let my giant leaps and strident steps

Show my true love, my dear
        My gentle touch
Touch me too, a soft delicious
        Kiss
Embrace and hug my being in a
        World like this
Come, come closer
        Touch my soul
Mingle with my spirit
Reawaken love and closeness
        Not forsaken
Let me glide, spin, turn and twist
        By the angel and stars
Oh joy, oh gladness
        I've been loved and kissed
Instilled with hope
        There will be so much more


## Self-Medicate

Silence, isolation, meditation
Like powerful pills that stimulate the brain

Try it
In space to endless horizons
When you return to earth
Maybe wonder if all is still real
Bordering, conjuring, a touch of insanity
Or "pilly" profusion of confusion

## Alone

I am alone
Solid, mass,
Crescendo of music
Surrounded by pictures, books
Dark, gloomy no one cares or looks
Too many things
More things
The loneliness I feel
The loneliness is real
Helpless in place
Immovable, take space
Inanimate, grey shade
Millennium my fate

So come and fetch me
Free me – break my habit chains
Stir me, catch me
Shine, dine and fine me
Chisel me alive
Desire, thrive
But do not clone
Then both of us will be alone

Breathe new life and undo
I'll respond - I do need you
Transform, perhaps change
New overtures and plans arrange
Meanwhile I am still alone

Tired, throw me back again
Relive the element including rain
Set me in place
Solid, face the sun and grace
It's easier to move mountains

Change the course of rivers
Than change people
I am still alone in this place.


## Contemplation Expands

Contemplation expands
To the furthest corners of the universe
Of the mind, of vision – of projection
I'm almost ready to get up
Stretch realities, sense my funny bone
Vegetate, more creative sparkle
Visions, ideas now into place
Watch out the final power of gestation
Finished activity
Many men produce
Experiment - new birth
Can we make up?
How fast will we heal – to heal we will

# Battery

the battery                           (slowly)
                                       drains

          partially    sustained

                        not enough

   a choking,    shattered

                         muttering   tick   tack


      the engine won't kick over

                              in anger I contemplate

delirious,    frustrating   fate

                       I sit                    think

no   (1)      (2)   blame

                   the battery is dead

   Stone dead   - dead ----dead

Go – buy a new one

            But let me keep my heart

# A Day in Numbers

The day      three-fourths done
Discourse with friends, much fun
The western sky, bright setting sun
6    valuable hours towards midnight
7    before the day is gone

New fragrant blend of roses here to view
A secret eerie peace dispels a witch's brew
The same tranquility stored with new hope
I conjure common half-day      how to cope

There is no hidden war, no imminent distaste
The busy hours flee as I now race
No let up, no reprieve
A touch of doubt, mustered with wisdom and belief
So soon the dance, the feast will end
As I stare into moonlit night and
Hold the hand of my dear friend
Soothing fatigue with sleepiness does blend

This day is special
As is every other day
Exciting visit here on earth
I'm here – short time      I hope to stay!

## Eagle Spread

Eagle spread
I, early morn – in bed
Fuzzy thoughts soon focus sharp
Contemplate painlessly as
I stare at the green bedroom ceiling
Eyes open now awake, alert

The night before
(or could it have been  half century before?)
Has left its toll
What crazy misbegotten mischief
Was my role?

Not ambitious
Hypnotic, lazily transfixed
The blankness of the ceiling's cream color calms
Like the sameness of the prison wall
Says escape, move the body – up – up
I lie, I stare – solid – immobile except my eyelids

From rest, tranquility
Unto the tense stage of upcoming events
Of today's demands, of chores, of duty
Uncompromising agony
While I still lie like a dead stone
Transfixed, eagle spread, painless position

Why weigh the thoughts
Of yesterday's impurity
Real or imagined
Did I really do that?

The simple bell in rhythm
Cajoles – time to move, get up!

Enough dream pictures – move!
Demands a sad continuum of lifetime of routine
My thoughts so dreamy
The world so real


### Cycle of Life

Complex from birth
Baby's bar graph radical, not mirth
Embryo of innocent child
Octogenarian decaying mind confused, wild.

Toiling peasant , dutiful provider
Primitive gear
Eke out existence – freedom rider
Nature's child      without fear.

To all: Life just a game
Playing with toys innocent without blame
Relish the newness
Win, lose, assess.

Out of nature
Part of nature
Within nature
Nature's toys.

Hear the laugh, the cry
Anguish as the game goes dry.
Smile, play with zest
Win or lose, game, not a test.

In innocent cocoon

Into maturity
Adult, adjust to life so soon
See world in glory and impurity


Experience the world of many pleasures
Close to the abyss of the many deaths
Miraculous resurrections ready to confront
Like warrior choose
Eternal battles win and loose.

Aged, survivor, soul-searched
On death precipitance now perched
Outlived, feeble fraught with innocence
Play last few games with dire consequence

Cycle of child and old age



### Destiny's Gift

We give gifts and receive them
Many times each day
As we do intercede
Destiny holds sway

As members of world's tribe

It's now the time
To pick the fruit so rich and ripe

The other side of nothing

    Is your vision

How you perceive, how you believe

       How you retrieve

Green winding landscaped valley

        Crevices filled with icy snow jagged into
                the sky


The other side of nothing

Just hours since the baby breathed

    Into the world, hungry crying

The tenor and soprano voice brilliantly

    Shattering the auditorium

The other side of nothing

Bleeding profusely from an accident

    How lucky to be alive

The other side of nothing

Elated, just passed the course test

    Always yearning learning earning

The other side of nothing

Can be nothing

    Until you open your eyes

    The other side of nothing is

    Something – momentous

## So Close, So Far

I am in a strange land
Just 200 miles from home
It's the atmosphere you understand
Feeling different, an unsure bland

Placid, scenic, emerald lake
It's the friendly waitress I do partake
It's the water, music, customs that are so different
New scenes – same stars
The planets twinkle, Pluto – Mars

Yet in the same state
Same language  - different words
Or different interpretation
Outlooks interesting representation

In my cocoon of home I felt safe
Now away, varied new images I crave
Most men not born to hibernate
All seek adventure if they rate

Same mental state and insulation
Simply can't escape
Yet we can change venue, location
Radiate in our new environment with great sensation

It's our body, form of our shell
That may not now adjust so well
When to laugh, when to cry
When to be open, honest
Test each white lie

I'm only a short distance from home
The sea of newness cast a shame

Does this belong to me – a cloud of foam
Yet I – each one here does have a name.

Yet I'll adopt
My curiosity has never stopped
Nor has yours dear reader
Let's adventure and enjoy our latest leader

Dazzle mind with feast and frolic
Noise and smell of food and alcohol
Quaint furniture hug and carouse
Celebration joyous, fair game, tame

Once returned to my own home
I'll never be the same

*Within*

Where do I find my inner peace
Where's the spirit, do I find my soul
When will fear, anxiety desist and seize
How can I heal, make me more whole

It is within the energy and brain
It's in our imagination
It's in the experience and sensation we sustain
A complex self-fulfilling operation

It treads on expansive dreams
It's man's god-like potential
It's virulent, turbulent exploding at the seam
Explored, digested, consequential

It's deep within the "Id" and I
Evolve the feeling, vision to perceive
It's acting chromosomes genes that try
Shape, guide, persuade the giant monsters in
            What we do believe

Stay earthy, measure momentary worth
Enjoy the things that work and please
Not grapple with the future, failure
            Common curse
Erase some worry, active in my search
            Of inner peace

All life toward goals
Which paces, integrates and blends
A treadmill of the soul
All life transforms and has many ends

*Last Leaves*

Bare branches
L
O
With reddish brown
      Wafting last dying leaves
Ice cold wind announceS
                  E
                  A
                  S
                  O
                  Never more
Flutter to the ground
      Decay as all in a cycle
            Back to dust
The sturdy tree trunk
Naked awaiting spring with me
Precious budding season

*Lusty Lips*

I sensually glide my fingers
Over my lips
Soon swollen, stimulating, sexed up
Different from kissing
Full of hormones
Try it      let yourself go ...
See what you are missing
And please, don't blame me.

## *Two Watches*

two watches fixed

two on my arm  to test

both tell          the same time

Tight as the arm does move with little rest

The watches but one minute      a-
part

time pieces      exact      look  fashionable      smart

Steady shine    in silence move  in rhythm

unlike the beating of my
heart

exact, a fact    quiet, take    little space

minute hand demonstrative, alive

As I look anxious:      " Is it time?"

Next step – next place – next call

Or darn the watches    must leave = too much
to haul

Seconds to hours      cut from life

two watches at one time

I can tell the difference

Must go must go  - no time

## Making a Mistake

To make a serious mistake
In innocence and not even know
Is an ego downer and personal blow

It wasn't your selection
You are not God nor all perfection
What's done is done
There's no repeating

We all have flaws, still we are good
Accept yourself, did all you could

## Winners and Losers

Every day someone wins and loses
Someone gambles, someone chooses
Someone freely wages, bets
Only poor losers have regrets

My pride, is the fun and joy of winning
With nerves and stamina today a new beginning
Clever, I calculate, risk, confront
The trophy of victor, me, I hope I will be donned

My challenge, dare, with guts I enter the gambling cage
And after struggle may lose the battle in a stormy rage
I laugh it off, jump into the fury once anew

With bluff and brilliant play, my enemy unglued
And with new win subdue the urge to gloat
It's just a game of risk as I toss in my stormy boat
Not cured, not broke, addicted I venture in without delay
Excited for the new most challenging day
Like all who trade too many stocks or drink or sex – addicted
In wanton self-destruction, I too, non-restricted

Bordering on the insane, I feel that sooner or later- win or lose
Victory will come my way  - as I, the gambler, pick and choose


### Amongst the Creatures

My tongue does echo English but not Greek
In most effective tone, direct and not oblique
Do it – it stammers – now – do it right
Absent my determination, cowardice is not in sight

The thought in motion does direct act
Deal with my maker seals my pact
Why am I - what am I to date, to berate?
Challenge the world and challenge fate

I, man funny looking, do not resemble bird
A dog sniffs up at me as if I were a nerd
I much prefer a fancy car and special seats on a plane
I, stringy, awkward will never be the same.

I, with too long and strident legs
Bulging stomach, most peculiar sex
A torso, more so with a hairy head
I delay, delay and hate to go to bed

I daresay do my task, know to build
Build planes, fancy cars where one gets killed
Run and gallivant, talk in awkward way
Fence and banter – waste away the day

Live in my box called house
Place of freedom, food and to carouse

I, the alter ego of the whale
Consume my fish, I tell my tale
I, the bison, roam with sleepers
Too busy to do coke, exchange with creepers

See monsters rule the world
Blast each other up, grenades hurled
Steal each other's land
With innocence atomic bombs you send

Human, among the earthlings
Special chosen
One day smell roses, next glaciers frozen
Why not acclimate
Within reason learn to do as I please
As creatures special live together in peace.

## This is the Day

Boring – hell no!

        One day blends into another

A ticking unrelenting chain,     unending

Ever moving       As heart throbs, tongue tastes block

So percolate, circulate

        Rejuvenate

Time ever moving,     busy involved vacation recreation

Impregnates all it touches - Evolves   evolution

        Into order, disorder – discordant – real

Rattling earthquakes  torrents of cascading rain

Erosion, explosion       Fire, acid air dust

Life on a balance bar

        Tossed cooked, digested

Regurgitated, struggling

        To breathe, heave

Say *This was my day. This is my day!*

Expended,   never ended

Until suddenly a jolt

Vision, recognition

Shaken – awaken – demand of action

I lose my balance and my grip

Only with sanity, sheer will feel now reborn

The meaning of the moment regained

Only to be lost in the vicissitudes

Of time


## *Thank Myself*

We often thank the wrong person
The right person should be us
Without us no perception
No miracles
We are the receivers
The beneficiary
I thank heaven as I thank myself

## A Pedestal

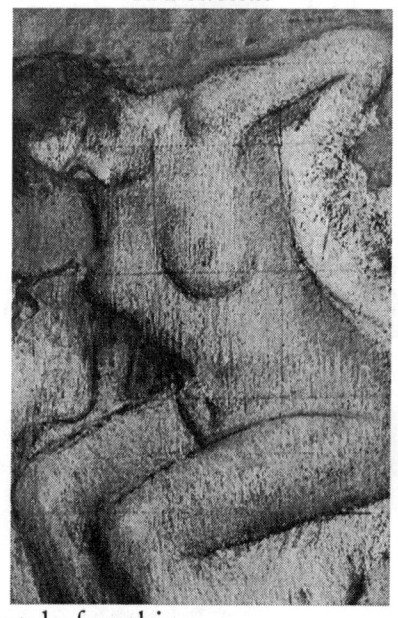

I stand on a pedestal of nothing
Naked, I own nothing, something to behold
Exposed, misshapen, braggart scold
Hard to discipline, free spirit old
Young for love, for touch and kiss
There on that pedestal I postulate
Exclaim, pontificate
The world on fire, flame, excitement, desire
Mind and tongue search prancing beauty
Array of faces pain the eye
Smiling salvation etched in stone, I cannot cry
The couples in arms
Entwined lovers in alarm
Discovered, disrobed
Love is eloped
Tasted all the yearning
      Of each body, odor, breath
      Hypnotize, mesmerized
      Hormone dominates

Each act discovered, surprised
Searching more, more
Score, adore
More to allure
The monster longing does not invade
Each sensation a fancy moment
Never to be reborn the same
Ah, love, beauty with exhaustion
The battery is weak
Thought, sensation, blessings do run deep
How precious
The art of love


## Opening Up

so often
                    in our business

        our hearts
                            show pangs of loneliness


who listens
            who accepts the way I am
                        who can I confide in


        touch
                without        judgement

let me empty fear
replacement by faith
new confident

first I have to open up

pure honesty

the rest will follow

*The Seeds of Poetry*

Heroic, read my poem to admire
Of grace, deeds, envy, ire
Of loves, devotion, anguish blind
Of losing faith, of hope and mind

Yet within each phrase
Within the rhythm and tumultuous pace
There is rebirth, renewed deep dedication
Mind, eyes wide open a new regeneration

For watered colored buds sprout out of splendid plant
Too frail, we failing creatures ere but do recant
A poem can transform into gigantic engines
Bring tear or anger acid pain in disposition
Cry out to mankind touching all our senses
Word pictures eloquent in their rendition
Phrases ignite the mind for change for doing good
Gather the undecided, lost and conquer dreams
Into a true and most diverse new brotherhood

Transform loud prayer into visible deed
Teach, admire magic plant reborn
From tiny seed
So that the stranger, sick, indolent arrive
Entranced, invigorated into our new life

Give me the pleasure of a ripe, rich poem any day
Before the thunderous avalanche of daily deed holds sway
Let me escape and ape into the poetry of daily life
With grandeur entice brain and dream stay ready, rife


## Different Beds

Can you recall how many
Different beds you slept in
No wonder you are not
The same person

## In the Senses

Stream of word consciousness lure and demand
Like earthquake test     things that remain and  stand
In rhythm poetic phrases hibernate, regurgitate
And link in sentence to resuscitate
The deadly words did spew
Cling in my memory like glue
The quake that shatters heaven and when complete
All through
Disaster!

Although our lifeblood often sucked
Fanfare and motto - reconstruct
New energy, resurgence of my iron will
Creative and determined goal to fill
Immense destruction     costly to rebuild
Calamity – some survive, too many killed.

Message delivered honest and demanding
Positive injection, language so commanding
Awareness with affection for all to see
So I love you, the world and even me

When I hear, or smell, and simply taste
The sound, the word in new directions phased
Blueprints oral, contracts build with touch of modernity
Futuristic, solid, within the confines of eternity

Religions, revolutions moved by tongue and sword
Rooted in fairness, harmony compromise in that accord
Byline is vision of deep love, its scent, taste and sounds
Mingled with armour and cupid all around

This message of the mind
Translated into action of its kind
And in this delegation to rebuild
On sound foundation ere we sink in silt

Rebuild the temples, towers, institution
No one said it would be easy, new our resolution
I toast all who participate
Pray and revere before it is too late.

### The Angel

Imagine!
Escape to splendor
Mountain top resort
Isolated yet 21$^{st}$ Century
All modern conveniences
Vistas of horizon meeting mountain crest
Hue of grays and greens
Balanced against the azure sky
The lake, the bed of rainbow flowers
The bluebird, squirrel teasing
View, scenes, comfort

Surround sound
Lounge chairs, books
Gourmet delicacies
Vacation wonder

Warmth
Idyllic, peaceful isolated

A time to contemplate
Listen to birds and music
Read to hearts content
Let the brain rest or explode to nirvana

Housekeeper on premises
The path, the pool, frolic

What a springboard for life
What infinite possibilities
Write, converse, absorb, love

Meditate, concentrate

Then a knock at the door
An angel enters
To make paradise
Reality
Welcome
Let me greet you
With kisses
With hugs

Yes, much of this is real
Will you prove it to me?

### Between Dreams

waking     blue

sky

with a yawn

too tired now


shut my     (eye(s))     again

shut  out  the  world

for a few more winks

let my soul     get

nourished


mend     and     heal

before demanding day

divides and isolates

into a thousand

crescendos

I, the strumpet

of the puppeteer

ready to ascend from the
netherworld

109

## This Last Smile

I am        a hazard
   To my health

Long ago amazed by some wealth

         Now to think of food        sex   with joyful
abandonment
   So much              excitement              can't      relax

So much beauty  - so much life – natures colors mesmerize

Too much in the system
                              Makes it shake like      a cows

                    u        r
                  t    e
                  t

Even          when I can't
      Breathe     in rhythm

         I go do all that I enjoy
                              So when the undertaker
remove

My        s                              e
            m              l
                  i

   I had my fun        through all the miles

Please leave my smile for all to see

## Drama-rama

In rasping irony

I decry *too much theatre*

After I awake, theatre

All day action

Night transformed   (again)
          on stage

None of this is an act

It's more like a comedy – my drama


Tragedy behind the curtain – not time yet

It's real, I feel it

The puppet actor

The dog barked          then bit

Car accident          buckets of rain – he will live

You the audience          a participant

Comic tragedy of life


(I just happened to be the protagonist)

We are the players of each day

right now  ready to attach to fence  with heavy hand

not by choice

unless new scene

transforms into uncharted course

tense – inviting  grimace – tears -  lunatic discourse

as nature's fury races

to the final curtain

*Rapture*

Heavy breath abated
Coitus, unison, rapture
All in one
Exhausted, all relaxed
Had a game of love and sex
So much fun
So blessed
I need a rest
All the same
It was just a game

## *Blueprint*

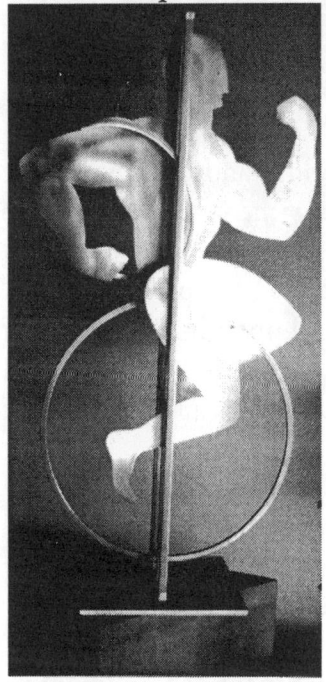

I – you everyone's on stage
Drama, comic world theater script our page
Innocent, self-involved, we play our dramatic part
I – you painfully searching, with our mind and brittle heart

Into battle I cross swords with banker and kings
In dream, with valor jump and toss my ring
Into the current circus of life so full of dare
I clown, comic turn, create and I do care

Calmer waters, I heap my kisses warm and soft
My touch strong stimulant will takes me soon aloft
High, distant over the expanse of our infinite earth
From distance ponder, quiver, pray what is all this worth?

When, at last, for dinner I arrive
The hurried husband, or exulted wife

Warmly greet children, relatives and friends
Fatigued, sincere but worn, too tired to hold hands

An extra surge of energy renew
To stay in disbelief, seek honesty and truth
Help house, community and church
Unseen trophy on my mantelpiece does lurch

To help the old, the sick, the poor
To give my wisdom, hope allure
With self-searching, self-educate
To live life as it is and call a spade a space

Relieved in thanks, leave when I retire
To bed, to rest with those that I admire
To stay the course of culture where I live
Receive the beautiful, to share and give
To stay the course without remorse
Read, stretch for the advent of tomorrow
For my life is too precious as each day I borrow
Twice daily stop to thank the lord
For life today I can afford
Sometimes try the unconventional – the absurd
Eyes, ears wide open, with all things alert
Time's running out so fast
In the mirror's face I see my age
Must say good bye at last.

## Twilight Age

Twilight in my old age
In room alone
The outside noise muffled
Sedentary – in chair – in thought
Scan today's excitement
I lapse in thought – sleepy
With visions so alive of past
School, family I set the stage
To wile away last days
Waiting for the phone

Self-sufficient
No one to bother me
Nor do I make any claims
When you are over 65 you paid your fee
Live, enjoy the sunshine and rain

Can blast radio or TV
Can join a dozen clubs
Can look in mirror and see myself
Devour books, reading time never stops

I make my bed
Prepare my meal
Visit my yuppie kids
Often, in the quiet, lonely I do feel

It's my choice to live with borders and wires
The patio, the car waiting
Creative silence most divine
Few at the house are ever congregating

Even in crowds, at work
Loneliness persists

Friend says: "Let's go for a walk."
O.K.

Introspective, lonely clerk
The negative, I'm never missed

So as you age
Chart last course
Interact as wisdom's sage
Backtrack with remorse

We're born helpless, dependant
Proud master our realm
Old age survivor of a tough descendent
Take charge, master at the helm

You're free
The world is waiting for you

No cost, no fee
Get up, go out, do it
O.K., O.K. I told you
I am coming.

## Open Wounds

I wailed for years

                my mind

perspective, meaning

          changed

                       more

towards kind

  timed what I say

          goodbye, I'll go away

shall return

          to shake the pillars of foundation

over-confidence

          can lead to open wounds

            bleed to death

or in the act

          and deep belief

                rebirth - we heal to

venture

With each exciting action

                change the scenery

## *Burial Day*

I ask myself most poigned, I do grieve
How can a shining star's life be so brief
Right in the midst of harvest and bloom
Dead, still and buried in a tomb

Man's omnipotence measured
        by his life and deed
                on earth

Only by doing, shaping, will we
        barely know what all is
                worth

All by G'd and space is finite, has an
      end
On this moment's thought
      movement can now depend

Do not expect the world to coddle you
      forever
For only you can now direct, pull the
      lever

Tow to eternity

### *Free Flow*

Free flow my thought
I feel crucified
Caught
Honest, stupid spilled word
I didn't mean it THAT WAY
Overflowed the spirit
Spontaneous judgement wrong
Hurt
So sorry
So careful when you free flow
Sound of words chained, linked
Like my mind is free-falling
Out of control
My words the seeds, dangerous
That I sow in audio or written
Water, fertilize and keep
Words smitten or can do bidding
Utter thoughts, I'm hemmed in

The tongue precedes the mind
Free flow, kind and unkind
Once in the atmosphere
Can't put it back into the bottle
But let the spirits explode
In every direction
Someone exposed,
Misinterprets or adores
You said      you said it
Now must regret it
Didn't mean it
I apologize


## Ritual of Sleep

The ritual of going to bed
            is remarkable unique
It is an abdication, celebration of
            the day of peace at night
            A celebration – pure delight
It is to fade out, meet the angels
            be it now or nevermore
            No one to judge or keep the score
It is to celebrate body, rest, reprise
Kiss, giants    close my  eyes
            become helpless
            innocent dreaming like  babies
Punishment or reward for harm
            lived the day
            Advent of peace – soothe the alarm
We rejoice or dread the day
At night, sleep is healing, soothing
            innocent, without guilt or

obligation
No beginning, end or ration
As the screen of vivid pictures
the living and dead
events all spring to life
Lulling us to sleep
Into the ecstasy of numbness I do leap
Partake in giant dreams
Dreams, pictures of the universe
Kaleidoscope of color, people, events, puppets and pets
all dancing in our complicated heads
The body within so consumed
Those intervene, disturb will soon be doomed.
Remarkable how the human machine
must rest.
And with the angels our spirit blessed


## D Day

D Day, remarkable
Hit the beachhead where thousands died
Saved my freedom, my pride
Most of all you see
Twist of history
I, a soldier, almost there
It could have been me

## Accessories

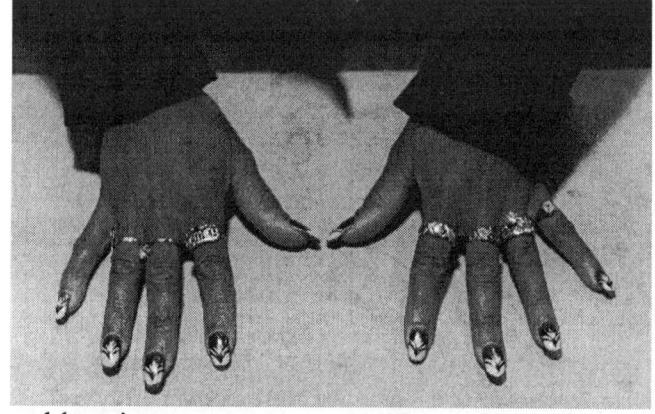

my golden ring

                is my companion

      as is my watch

                        dressing now

(one) hand
(one) arm

                My hand – my arm are true beholders

                    listening to every word I      utter

absorb every sound

                        to deep secret thoughts

        my appendages

                are my witnesses

122

(thank God they hear
but cannot talk)

absorb        keep silent

      most of what I say is nonsense anyhow


            Right     That is why you hear me loud
and clear!



## It Never Happened

The green rolling meadow
Interspersed with foliage, trees
Casting an eerie shadow
Where starving women walked, would freeze
Anne Frank in youth enslaved, decayed
The British freed the living skeletons too late.
I and my daughter Judy witnessed the gruesome mounds and
tombs
5,000, 10,000 buried than 5000 – 10,000 more and more and
more
Among new blooms
Bergen-Belsen
IT NEVER HAPPENED.

Remnants on French, Austrian and Germans interred
In southern Vichy France
Uncle Karl, My father Siegfried, Uncle Walter all had earned
the Iron Cross – death – torture their reward - absurd
Prisoners of the SS net and Himmler's plans
Disease, starvation, a year or so – Walter died

Siegfried, my dad, with visa shipped to Martinique
Uncle Karl, in cattle car to Auschwitz in the night
Camp Gurs
IT NEVER HAPPENED

Steinheim, Westphalia
Weils, my family rooted for hundreds of years
Orders arrest 70 year old Ida, grandmother, loyal matron
Innocent believer, part of 12 million tears
The ovens of Auschwitz her reward and patron
Old family farmhouse, family meadowland confiscated
Years later I received $1,000 compensation
Auschwitz
IT NEVER HAPPENED

Some did escape with soul so jarred
Branded, naked, determined to rebuild
I, 12 years old, in Chicago spared
The anguish, pain of childhood now unfilled

An orphan searching for identity
In a sea of freedom without life-savers
To carry cross and torch and memory and hurt
Remnant, rebuilt, grandchildren that thrive
Serious, cognizant, unsure, alert, still very much alive
IN FREEDOM
IT NEVER HAPPENED

I mourn the gypsies, disabled, protesters and priests
Nine million tortured, starved who died
I, angry, pained, stalked by those civilized beasts
Amongst them 1.5 million children – ghosts - few torturers
Were tried the children still live in my heart
I - you, invisible – seared
Could be the flame branded number on our arm
Can't you see the child's wide and searching eyes

How can we fathom such cruel, calculated extermination
In God's name someone and heaven knew
Later: "We're are sorry, We'll pay reparation"
How could the world stand by without a clue?
Pearl Harbor – defend freedom, save our nation
I lived, I lived, I was sixteen years old
The death camps, the forced labor,
The continent under the thump of the master race
The ominous smell from burned flesh, gassed bodies
When it happened the world knew, but I was never told
Someone had to know? Where is man's conscience?
Cultured civilized reverted to the basest forms of bestiality
Incomprehensible – is it still happening?
I still can't understand,
I still can't comprehend
Can you?
Some say: "IT NEVER HAPPENED."

## A Formula

Faith coupled with deed
Are the mortar
That brings success

## A Poet's Creation

poets in leisure
        the mind     free

        creative

  words     lines              flow

combined thoughts    GROW

    notions
   emotions
        of...   ...things
            ...worlds
            ...love
            ...regret
More word pictures  in all hues and shapes

   To tease the mind
   Framed, fragmented
   Exciting, exploding

  copulation      transmittance
  confrontation with your mate

rhyme    verbs    syllables on wings

          descriptive   adjectives
words    fashion soon   transcend

        by readiness   absorbed

Care – conscience – so unique
   each figure dressed   different
Transferred into the creative mind

## Your Gift

The silver-plated shoe horn gift
Engraved in love gives me a lift
A symbol, token, almost divine
I think of you, I quiver and I pine

I thank you for this lovely weight
Its beauty I will highly rate
As I use it, I say in whispering tone
Thanks, as I hold, share and call it my own

I thank you for kind tender words
When you are gone, I pout, I miss you and it hurts
Until we meet again, it's such delight
Your grace, your charm so perfect and so right

My gift to you is love's embrace
You are my chosen in the busy race
When our bodies merge both in deep pleasure
There is a joy, grandeur without measure

So stay with me, and love me true
As greater friendship will ensue
Each step fantastic, beyond sensation
Each touch, each stroke, each lick
An endless elation
How lucky!

*When*

(between)
cooking the dream

of gamble
of fortune foresworn

finite, exact

when the wines are rich and  ripe

when the essence is  time

heaping profit          cousin luck

into a regulated
order

Tongue, tingling     licking, gurgling

Fragrance, alcohol

Numbing mind and spirit in love

In compassion - delirious

when will I have

my turn?

## Must I Decide?

And in this turbulence of mind
Perplexed my nature all but kind
In deep frustration I'll sort it out
I want to do the right thing
That's what it's all about
I must decide for sure
Thank God I am not perfect or so pure
O.K. O.K., hear my decision and my choice
We'll all now share and implement
Singularly in a most united voice

## Just Be Sure

Simple     read me

     I love you

       You love me

   So exciting

      Beginning age      space

Sex      gender

      I greet you

         You greet me

    Two specks on a planet

    Lost somewhere in cosmos

        Just be sure

to say goodbye

As I will say

     I love you too

## How Many Endings?

How many endings

        does each story contain   ?

    as many
        as time
            allows

   perhaps infinite

        Vivid imagination – new perspective

           until with a devastating thud
                no more

brain dead

        the end of pain

        the end of feeling

the beginning of nirvana

        eternal is the blessing

           only in our heart, mind

  his being
      lives on

        his time has come

*Give and Take*

In my love for you and me
I owe you nothing
You are not indebted to me
Yet I owe you
Everything
You a New World that created me
You owe everything to me
Until my body melts
Mixes with gasses and the soil
To let my heart beat
Enrich my mind
With life explosive nature
Every kind
To dip my thought
Into each new idea
Experience, move on
To bake, make, shape
To test, try escape
Start anew
My mind, a world of its own
Limitless, amazing, not fazing
A new perspective
Thanks to you

## At Day's End

It's late dear
So good night
Wish you
Good, restful slumber
Think not of toil
Of all exasperating
Convoluting, diabolical
Confrontations of the day
Mostly calm
Routine, impersonal
Relax, breathe slowly
You did your shopping
Your hugs, your meals
Now the mind needs rest
Restore, recharge
Good, bad, indifferent
Now, bedtime, helpless
Cook up dreams
Reflect on love, touch
Think of warmth, of friendship
Darkness calms the spirit
As slowly, eyes tired

Up too early
I smile
I breathe, slow      deep
I know I will awake
If not
I did have a full day
Even a full life
Good night

Other Titles by Arthur Weil:

Life, Love and Gems That Shine ($8.00)
Exploding Mind or (Not Over the Hill Yet) ($5.00)
Poetry is for Sissies ($5.00)


All books ordered directly will have a 25% discount with no shipping costs. Contacts can be made by e-mailing aweil444@aol.com. or calling (510) 654-5626. Books can also be ordered through amazon.com.

These books make excellent gifts and are autographed by the author.